1000 Positive Affirmations for Women

A Collection of Empowering affirmations to Ignite your Potential

Harry Wilde

Copyright © 2023 by Harry Wilde

All rights reserved. No part of this publication may be reproduced, stored or transmitted in any form or by any means, electronic, mechanical, photocopying, recording, scanning, or otherwise without written permission from the publisher. It is illegal to copy this book, post it to a website, or distribute it by any other means without permission.

Contents

1	Introduction	1
2	Self-Love and Self-Acceptance	3
3	Body Positivity and Self-image	8
4	Empowerment and Personal Strength	15
5	Confidence and Success	22
6	Relationships and Connection	27
7	Career and Professional Growth	33
8	Mindfulness and Emotional Well-being	40
9	Personal Growth and Continuous Learning	47
10	Balance and Well-being	54
11	Gratitude and Abundance	61
12	Conclusion	68

1

Introduction

Are you ready to go on a journey that will enable you to embrace your inner strength, conquer self-doubt, and display confidence? Welcome to "1000 Positive Affirmations for Women," a book that will boost your soul, spark your potential, and lead you to a life of optimism and abundance.

This book is a treasure trove of inspirational affirmations that have been carefully crafted to celebrate the spirit of womanhood and encourage personal progress in all aspects of your life. Each segment, divided into 10 separate categories, focuses on a different facet of your being, delivering a wide selection of affirmations to suit your individual path.

The advantages of practicing positive affirmations are profound. By intentionally incorporating them into your daily routine, you might feel a rise in self-confidence, self-esteem, and determination to achieve your ambitions. Affirmations have the power to reshape your perspective, eliminate limiting beliefs, and allow you to reach your full potential. They act as a constant reminder of your innate value and the endless opportunities that await you.

To get the most out of this book, I recommend that you actively engage with its content. Repeat each affirmation with intention and belief, as if it were a holy chant. Choose a peaceful period in your day, make a sacred space for yourself, and let these affirmations sink into your awareness. Allow them to permeate into your soul, nurturing your spirit and reshaping your vision of yourself and the world around you.

Whether you read this book from cover to cover or just dip into it when you need a boost of energy, remember that you have the key to unlocking your own greatness. By adopting these affirmations and implementing them into your everyday life, you are taking a significant step toward personal growth, self-discovery, and empowered living.

Let's begin this inspiring journey together, one affirmation at a time.

2

Self-Love and Self-Acceptance

The chapter will take you on a transforming journey of accepting your true self and nurturing a profound feeling of love and acceptance. You will learn to appreciate your unique talents, let go of self-judgment, and cultivate a deep love for yourself, just as you are, through powerful affirmations.

1. I love and accept myself unconditionally.
2. I embrace my unique qualities and celebrate my individuality.
3. I am worthy of love, happiness, and all the good things in life.
4. I radiate confidence and inner beauty.
5. I am enough, just as I am.
6. I deserve love and respect.
7. I am proud of who I am becoming.
8. I am worthy of self-care and prioritize my well-being.
9. I trust and believe in myself.
10. I release the need for approval from others and embrace

my authentic self.
11. I am beautiful inside and out.
12. I speak kindly to myself and treat myself with compassion.
13. My self-worth is not determined by external validation.
14. I choose to focus on my positive qualities and strengths.
15. I am confident in expressing my needs and boundaries.
16. I am worthy of pursuing my dreams and goals.
17. I deserve happiness and fulfillment.
18. I deserve love and a healthy relationship.
19. I am grateful for my body and all that it does for me.
20. I nourish my body with love and make choices that honor its well-being.
21. I am at peace with my past and embrace a bright future.
22. I trust in the divine wisdom within me.
23. I forgive myself for any mistakes I have made and grow from them.
24. I let go of comparison and celebrate my own journey.
25. I am a magnet for positivity and abundance.
26. I deserve success in all areas of my life.
27. I can overcome any challenge that comes my way.
28. I believe in my abilities and trust in my intuition.
29. I am proud of my accomplishments, big and small.
30. I am worthy of taking up space and voicing my opinions.
31. I am worthy of receiving love, kindness, and support from others.
32. I deserve joy and fulfillment in my relationships.
33. I attract healthy and uplifting relationships into my life.
34. I am surrounded by people who appreciate and respect me.
35. I am enough, regardless of my relationship status.
36. I deserve a partner who loves and supports me uncondi-

tionally.
37. I am open to giving and receiving love in its purest form.
38. I am whole and complete on my own.
39. I deserve success in my career and professional endeavors.
40. I trust in my abilities and have confidence in my work.
41. I am skilled and knowledgeable in my area of expertise.
42. I embrace challenges as opportunities for growth and learning.
43. I deserve recognition and rewards for my hard work.
44. I am confident in my ability to achieve my career goals.
45. I attract opportunities that align with my passion and purpose.
46. I am a valuable asset to any team or organization.
47. I am proud of my achievements and celebrate my progress.
48. I deserve financial abundance and prosperity.
49. I am open to receiving new opportunities and stepping out of my comfort zone.
50. I trust in the timing of my success and know that everything unfolds perfectly.
51. I am present at the moment and embrace the beauty of life.
52. I choose thoughts that uplift and empower me.
53. I release negative self-talk and replace it with positive affirmations.
54. I am grateful for all the blessings in my life.
55. I attract positivity and happiness into my day.
56. I deserve peace and inner harmony.
57. I am the creator of my own reality, and I choose to focus on the positive.
58. I trust that everything is working out for my highest good.
59. I am open to receiving guidance and inspiration from the

universe.
60. I deserve a life filled with love, joy, and fulfillment.
61. I release past hurts and embrace forgiveness.
62. I deserve a fresh start and new beginnings.
63. I am proud of my journey and the lessons I have learned.
64. I let go of my regrets and choose to learn from my experiences.
65. I deserve love, even with my imperfections.
66. I am grateful for the wisdom gained from life's challenges.
67. I trust in the process of life and have faith in my own resilience.
68. I am free to be myself and express my true emotions.
69. I deserve self-care and prioritize my mental and emotional well-being.
70. I choose to let go of self-judgment and embrace self-compassion.
71. I deserve rest and relaxation.
72. I attract positive and supportive friendships into my life.
73. I am surrounded by people who uplift and inspire me.
74. I am proud of the woman I am becoming.
75. I deserve happiness, success, and fulfillment in all areas of my life.
76. I trust that I am on the right path, even when things seem uncertain.
77. I am deserving of time and space to pursue my passions.
78. I am confident in expressing my thoughts and opinions.
79. I am open to receiving and giving love freely.
80. I deserve peace and serenity in my daily life.
81. I am grateful for my strengths, and I embrace my weaknesses with love.
82. I choose to see challenges as opportunities for growth and

transformation.
83. I deserve to express myself and embrace my creativity.
84. I am proud of my accomplishments and acknowledge my hard work.
85. I am deserving of self-acceptance, just as I am.
86. I am beautiful, both inside and out.
87. I trust in my own inner wisdom and intuition.
88. I deserve respect and to be treated with kindness.
89. I let go of the need to please others and prioritize my own happiness.
90. I am enough, exactly as I am at this moment.
91. I am deserving of success and prosperity in all areas of my life.
92. I am grateful for the abundance that surrounds me.
93. I am open to receiving and giving unconditional love.
94. I attract positive opportunities and experiences into my life.
95. I release fear and step into my power with confidence.
96. I deserve love and support from the universe.
97. I am worthy of all the happiness and joy life has to offer.
98. I am proud of my achievements and celebrate my growth.
99. I deserve love and admiration.
100. I am a strong, capable, and remarkable woman.

3

Body Positivity and Self-image

In this chapter, you will begin on a journey of self-discovery as you embrace the beauty of your body in all of its various forms. You will learn to accept and enjoy your body via uplifting affirmations, building a positive and empowered connection with yourself and your physical appearance.

1. My body is unique, beautiful, and deserving of love and care.
2. I embrace and celebrate my body's strength and resilience.
3. I am grateful for my body and all that it allows me to experience.
4. I release the need to compare my body to others and appreciate its individuality.
5. I nourish my body with love, nourishing foods, and gentle movement.
6. I am at peace with my body and accept it as it is at this moment.
7. I deserve to feel comfortable and confident in my skin.

8. My body is a vessel of love, joy, and positive energy.
9. I choose to focus on my inner beauty and radiate that outwardly.
10. I am worthy of self-care and prioritize my body's well-being.
11. I reject societal standards of beauty and define my worth.
12. I deserve respect and love, regardless of my body shape or size.
13. I embrace my imperfections and recognize that they make me unique.
14. I appreciate my body's ability to heal and regenerate.
15. I speak kindly to my body and treat it with love and compassion.
16. I am grateful for the senses and experiences my body allows me to enjoy.
17. I trust my body's wisdom and listen to its signals with love and understanding.
18. I am confident and comfortable expressing myself through my body.
19. I release negative thoughts about my body and replace them with affirmations of self-love.
20. I radiate beauty and confidence from within, regardless of external appearance.
21. I am proud of my body's accomplishments and milestones.
22. I deserve self-acceptance and love, regardless of any perceived flaws.
23. I choose to see the beauty in all body types and celebrate diversity.
24. I release the need for validation from others and embrace my self-worth.
25. I am deserving of love and affection, just as I am.

26. I am grateful for my body's ability to adapt and change.
27. I choose to nourish my body with positive thoughts and affirmations.
28. I am grateful for the miraculous ways my body supports my dreams and goals.
29. I deserve clothes that make me feel confident and comfortable.
30. I honor and respect my body's boundaries and needs.
31. I am worthy of self-expression through fashion, art, and personal style.
32. I am proud of my body's resilience and ability to bounce back from challenges.
33. I let go of unrealistic expectations and embrace my body's natural beauty.
34. I appreciate my body's curves and see them as a reflection of femininity and strength.
35. I deserve self-care practices that uplift and rejuvenate my body.
36. I love and accept every inch of my body, including its perceived flaws.
37. I am grateful for the energy and vitality my body provides me.
38. I choose to focus on my body's abilities and what it can accomplish.
39. I release the need for external validation and find confidence from within.
40. I deserve self-love and body acceptance every single day.
41. I embrace self-care rituals that make me feel good in my skin.
42. I am proud of my body's unique features and honor them as part of my identity.

43. I am grateful for the ways my body carries me through life's adventures.
44. I reject harmful societal beauty standards and embrace my definition of beauty.
45. I deserve self-compassion and forgiveness for any perceived shortcomings.
46. I choose to see my body as a masterpiece, perfectly imperfect in its way.
47. I nourish my body with positive thoughts, affirmations, and self-talk.
48. I appreciate my body's capacity to experience pleasure, joy, and connection.
49. I am confident and comfortable in my body, no matter the setting or situation.
50. I radiate confidence and beauty from within, illuminating the world around me.
51. I celebrate and love my body at every stage of life.
52. I am grateful for the miracles my body creates and sustains.
53. I deserve self-love, regardless of any perceived flaws or insecurities.
54. I release the need to hide or be ashamed of my body.
55. I deserve positive and loving relationships that honor and respect my body.
56. I honor my body's needs for rest, relaxation, and rejuvenation.
57. I am grateful for the wisdom my body holds and the messages it sends me.
58. I choose to focus on the things I love about my body, both inside and out.
59. I am confident and comfortable expressing my unique style and personal flair.

60. I deserve love and admiration, simply for being myself.
61. I appreciate the intricate beauty of every cell and organ in my body.
62. I let go of negative body talk and replace it with affirmations of self-love.
63. I am grateful for the ways my body supports me in pursuing my dreams and passions.
64. I embrace my body's natural rhythms and honor its cycles.
65. I deserve body-positive role models and communities that uplift and inspire me.
66. I choose to prioritize my body's well-being and make choices that support its health.
67. I am confident and comfortable in my body, allowing myself to fully participate in life.
68. I am grateful for the love and acceptance my body receives from those who matter most.
69. I embrace my body's feminine energy and radiate it with grace and confidence.
70. I deserve self-love and acceptance, no matter what stage of my journey I am on.
71. I am proud of the stories my body tells, the scars it bears, and the experiences it carries.
72. I release the need to conform to societal beauty standards and embrace my authentic self.
73. I am grateful for the ways my body communicates its needs and desires to me.
74. I deserve self-care practices that celebrate and nourish my body.
75. I choose to see my body as a temple of love, light, and positive energy.
76. I honor and appreciate my body's capacity for pleasure

and sensuality.
77. I am grateful for the support and love I receive from my body every day.
78. I embrace my body's unique proportions and recognize its beauty.
79. I am confident and comfortable in my body, allowing myself to take up space in the world.
80. I deserve body-positive media and messages that uplift and empower me.
81. I appreciate the diversity and strength of the female body in all its forms.
82. I release the need to strive for an unattainable ideal and embrace my version of beauty.
83. I am grateful for the ways my body adapts and changes to support my overall well-being.
84. I deserve self-love and acceptance, regardless of societal expectations.
85. I choose to see my body as a canvas for self-expression, adorned with love and creativity.
86. I am confident and comfortable in my body, appreciating its uniqueness and individuality.
87. I am grateful for my body's ability to heal and recover from illness or injury.
88. I embrace my body's natural cycles and rhythms, honoring its innate wisdom.
89. I deserve self-compassion and forgiveness for any negative self-talk or self-judgment.
90. I celebrate my body as a reflection of my journey, growth, and resilience.
91. I am grateful for the love and appreciation I receive for my body, both internally and externally.

92. I release the need to seek validation from others and embrace my self-worth.
93. I deserve self-care practices that honor and celebrate my body.
94. I choose to see the beauty in every part of my body, both visible and unseen.
95. I am confident and comfortable in my body, knowing that I am enough just as I am.
96. I am grateful for my body's ability to move, dance, and express itself.
97. I embrace my body's natural beauty, free from the constraints of societal expectations.
98. I deserve love and acceptance, regardless of any perceived imperfections.
99. I choose to see my body as a source of power, strength, and resilience.
100. I am grateful for the journey of self-love and body acceptance that I am on, knowing that every step is a beautiful victory.

4

Empowerment and Personal Strength

In this chapter, you will discover your boundless potential and learn how to use it to overcome difficulties and achieve success. You will nurture resilience, bravery, and unshakable conviction in your talents via motivating affirmations, allowing you to embrace your inner strength and create a life filled with purpose and accomplishment.

1. I am a powerful woman, capable of achieving anything I set my mind to.
2. I embrace my unique strengths and use them to create positive change in the world.
3. I trust my intuition and make decisions that align with my values and goals.
4. I am resilient and can overcome any challenges that come my way.
5. I deserve success and happiness in all areas of my life.
6. I am confident in my abilities and trust myself to handle any situation.

7. I deserve love, respect, and kindness from myself and others.
8. I am a leader, inspiring and empowering those around me.
9. I am worthy of achieving my dreams and pursuing my passions.
10. I embrace my authenticity and shine my light without fear or hesitation.
11. I can set healthy boundaries and prioritize my well-being.
12. I celebrate my accomplishments, big and small, and acknowledge my growth.
13. I am a magnet for positive opportunities, and I attract abundance into my life.
14. I release any self-limiting beliefs and step into my full potential.
15. I am strong, both physically and mentally, and can overcome any obstacle.
16. I deserve self-care and should prioritize my physical and emotional well-being.
17. I embrace change as an opportunity for growth and personal development.
18. I deserve success, and I allow myself to achieve greatness.
19. I am a source of inspiration and motivation for others.
20. I am grateful for my strengths and use them to create a positive impact in the world.
21. I trust myself to make decisions that align with my authentic self.
22. I deserve love and healthy relationships that support and uplift me.
23. I am confident in expressing my thoughts, ideas, and opinions.
24. I embrace challenges as opportunities for growth and

learning.
25. I am a beacon of light, spreading positivity and kindness wherever I go.
26. I deserve self-compassion and forgiveness for any mistakes or setbacks.
27. I can achieve a healthy work-life balance that nourishes my well-being.
28. I am worthy of success, recognition, and financial abundance.
29. I am an empowered woman, and my voice matters.
30. I am grateful for my unique qualities and the value they bring to the world.
31. I trust the journey of my life and know that everything happens for a reason.
32. I deserve self-love, self-care, and self-acceptance.
33. I am a warrior, and I face challenges with courage and determination.
34. I am a magnet for positive relationships and surround myself with supportive people.
35. I am confident in asserting my boundaries and saying no when necessary.
36. I deserve opportunities that align with my passions and purpose.
37. I am resilient, and I bounce back from setbacks stronger than before.
38. I believe in myself and my abilities to achieve greatness.
39. I am a force to be reckoned with, and I embrace my personal power.
40. I am grateful for my journey and the lessons it has taught me.
41. I am deserving of self-care, rest, and relaxation to recharge

my energy.
42. I can handle any challenges that come my way.
43. I embrace my uniqueness and celebrate the qualities that make me who I am.
44. I am confident in my abilities to learn and grow from every experience.
45. I deserve love and respect from myself and others.
46. I am empowered to make choices that align with my authentic self.
47. I am a source of inspiration and support for other women.
48. I am worthy of love, success, and happiness in all areas of my life.
49. I am brave, and I step outside of my comfort zone to pursue my dreams.
50. I am grateful for the strength and resilience that lie within me.
51. I trust my instincts and make decisions that serve my highest good.
52. I deserve self-expression and should embrace my unique voice.
53. I am a magnet for opportunities that align with my passions and purpose.
54. I am confident in my abilities, and I trust myself to navigate any situation.
55. I am worthy of success and achievement, and I celebrate my victories.
56. I am a catalyst for positive change in my life and the lives of others.
57. I am resilient, and I rise above any obstacles that come my way.
58. I embrace my flaws and imperfections, knowing they make

me beautifully human.
59. I deserve love, acceptance, and belonging.
60. I am grateful for my journey of personal growth and self-discovery.
61. I trust the process of life, and I surrender to the flow of the universe.
62. I deserve happiness and joy in all aspects of my life.
63. I can create a life that aligns with my dreams and desires.
64. I am confident in my abilities to overcome challenges and achieve my goals.
65. I am worthy of receiving abundance and prosperity.
66. I am an empowered woman, and I use my voice to create positive change.
67. I am resilient, and I bounce back from setbacks with grace and determination.
68. I embrace my uniqueness and appreciate the qualities that make me who I am.
69. I deserve self-compassion and self-care.
70. I am grateful for the lessons I have learned and the person I am becoming.
71. I trust in my ability to make decisions that align with my values and goals.
72. I deserve love, respect, and kindness from myself and others.
73. I am confident in expressing my needs and desires, knowing they are valid.
74. I am resilient, and I face challenges with strength and courage.
75. I am worthy of success, happiness, and fulfillment in all areas of my life.
76. I am a leader, and I inspire others with my actions and

words.
77. I can achieve my dreams and make a positive impact on the world.
78. I am empowered to take control of my life and create the future I desire.
79. I am deserving of self-love and self-acceptance, just as I am.
80. I am grateful for the unique talents and gifts that I share with the world.
81. I trust in my wisdom and make decisions that align with my truth.
82. I deserve a healthy and supportive relationship that uplifts me.
83. I am confident in my ability to overcome any obstacles that come my way.
84. I am resilient, and I learn and grow from every experience.
85. I am worthy of love and acceptance, exactly as I am.
86. I am empowered to speak up and advocate for myself and others.
87. I can achieve my goals and make my dreams a reality.
88. I deserve success, happiness, and abundance in all areas of my life.
89. I am a source of inspiration and strength for those around me.
90. I am grateful for my journey of self-discovery and personal growth.
91. I trust in my ability to navigate through life's challenges and come out stronger.
92. I deserve love, respect, and kindness from myself and others.
93. I am confident in my abilities and trust myself to make the

right decisions.
94. I am resilient, and I bounce back from setbacks with determination and grace.
95. I am worthy of success, happiness, and fulfillment in all areas of my life.
96. I am an empowered woman, and I use my voice to make a positive impact.
97. I can achieve my dreams and turn my visions into reality.
98. I deserve self-care and prioritize my well-being.
99. I am a beacon of light, inspiring and uplifting those around me.
100. I am grateful for the journey of self-love and self-acceptance that I am on.

5

Confidence and Success

Welcome to the chapter "Confidence and Success," where you'll learn about the transformational power of self-belief and uncover the secrets to realizing your greatest aspirations. You will nurture unshakable confidence, embrace your unique abilities, and release your entire potential to create a life of success and joy by using inspiring affirmations.

1. I am confident in my ability to achieve my goals.
2. I deserve success in all areas of my life.
3. I believe in myself and my potential to create a life I love.
4. I can overcome any challenges that come my way.
5. I trust my instincts and make choices that align with my values.
6. I am worthy of recognition for my accomplishments and talents.
7. I embrace failure as an opportunity to learn and grow.
8. I radiate confidence and attract positive opportunities.
9. I am fearless in the pursuit of my dreams and aspirations.

10. I have the power to create my own success story.
11. I release all self-doubt and embrace my inner strength.
12. I am resilient and bounce back from setbacks stronger than before.
13. I am open to receiving abundance and prosperity.
14. I believe in my unique skills and the value I bring to the world.
15. I deserve to be seen and heard for who I truly am.
16. I trust in my ability to make empowered decisions.
17. I am a magnet for opportunities that align with my passions.
18. I am confident in expressing my ideas and opinions.
19. I am unstoppable and capable of achieving anything I set my mind to.
20. I celebrate my achievements, big and small.
21. I attract positive and supportive people into my life.
22. I am worthy of respect and admiration for my accomplishments.
23. I am confident in networking and building valuable connections.
24. I step outside of my comfort zone to grow and expand.
25. I have a clear vision for my future and take inspired action towards it.
26. I trust that the universe is conspiring in my favor.
27. I am confident in presenting myself with authenticity and grace.
28. I embrace challenges as opportunities for personal growth.
29. I deserve recognition and praise for my hard work.
30. I am a strong and empowered woman.
31. I believe in my ability to achieve greatness.
32. I am confident in my skills and expertise.

33. I trust that my journey is unfolding exactly as it should be.
34. I am open to receiving guidance and support from mentors and role models.
35. I am worthy of financial abundance and prosperity.
36. I let go of comparison and focused on my unique path to success.
37. I attract opportunities that align with my passions and purpose.
38. I can handle any challenges that come my way.
39. I believe in my ability to turn obstacles into stepping stones.
40. I radiate confidence and inspire others around me.
41. I am deserving of the success and recognition I desire.
42. I am confident in asserting my boundaries and saying no when necessary.
43. I trust in the divine timing of my life's journey.
44. I am open to receiving support and guidance from others.
45. I am worthy of success and happiness in all areas of my life.
46. I release my self-limiting beliefs and embrace my limitless potential.
47. I am resilient and persevere through difficulties with strength.
48. I am a leader, and I inspire others through my actions and words.
49. I trust my intuition and make decisions with confidence.
50. I am grateful for the opportunities that come my way.
51. I can achieve my dreams and make a positive impact.
52. I believe in my ability to overcome any obstacles I face.
53. I am confident in my talents, skills, and abilities.
54. I attract abundance and success into my life effortlessly.

55. I radiate self-assurance and attract positive experiences
56. I am courageous and unafraid to take risks.
57. I release self-doubt and step into my power.
58. I deserve love, happiness, and fulfillment.
59. I embrace challenges as opportunities for growth and learning.
60. I am confident in my ability to handle whatever comes my way.
61. I trust in my inner wisdom to guide me toward success.
62. I am a magnet for opportunities that align with my purpose.
63. I believe in my potential to achieve greatness.
64. I am resilient, and I bounce back from setbacks with grace.
65. I celebrate my achievements and acknowledge my progress.
66. I am confident in my ability to handle difficult situations.
67. I attract positive and empowering relationships into my life.
68. I am worthy of success and all the abundance life has to offer.
69. I embrace my uniqueness and shine my light brightly.
70. I am enough, exactly as I am.
71. I trust that everything is working out for my highest good.
72. I am confident in my ability to overcome challenges.
73. I release self-criticism and embrace self-compassion.
74. I deserve all the opportunities that come my way.
75. I believe in my ability to create the life I desire.
76. I am open to receiving support and guidance from others.
77. I am confident in my decision-making abilities.
78. I can achieve my goals with ease and grace.
79. I trust in my ability to handle any situation that arises.

80. I radiate confidence and inspire those around me.
81. I am worthy of success and all the good things life has to offer.
82. I believe in my potential to make a positive impact on the world.
83. I am fearless in the pursuit of my dreams and aspirations.
84. I am confident in expressing my needs and desires.
85. I attract opportunities that align with my values and passions.
86. I trust in the process of life and surrender to its flow.
87. I deserve love, happiness, and abundance.
88. I am a powerful creator, and I manifest my desires with ease.
89. I embrace failure as a stepping stone to success.
90. I am confident in my ability to handle any challenge that comes my way.
91. I trust my intuition to guide me toward the right path.
92. I am open to receiving the support and help I need.
93. I believe in my ability to overcome any obstacles I encounter.
94. I am worthy of love, respect, and success.
95. I am confident in my ability to learn and grow.
96. I attract positive and uplifting people into my life.
97. I embrace my strengths and use them to achieve my goals.
98. I am resilient and bounce back from setbacks with determination.
99. I deserve all the opportunities that come my way.
100. I am confident, capable, and ready to seize the day.

6

Relationships and Connection

This chapter will take you on a journey of self-discovery while also deepening your relationships with others. You will create healthy relationships, nurture meaningful connections, and foster a sense of love, understanding, and support in all your interactions by using positive affirmations.

1. I attract loving and supportive relationships into my life.
2. I deserve a healthy and fulfilling connection.
3. I communicate my needs and boundaries with confidence and clarity.
4. I am open to giving and receiving love in all its forms.
5. I am worthy of a partner who cherishes and respects me.
6. I nurture and cultivate meaningful connections with others.
7. I attract friendships that inspire and uplift me.
8. I choose relationships that align with my values and bring me joy.
9. I am a magnet for positive and harmonious interactions.

10. I radiate love and compassion in all my relationships.
11. I deserve mutual respect and understanding in my relationships.
12. I attract romantic partners who appreciate and support me.
13. I embrace vulnerability and allow myself to be seen and heard.
14. I am open to receiving love and affection from others.
15. I create a safe and nurturing space for authentic connections to flourish.
16. I attract friendships that celebrate and empower me.
17. I deserve love and happiness in my relationships.
18. I let go of toxic relationships and make room for positive connections.
19. I trust my intuition to guide me toward healthy relationships.
20. I am grateful for the love and support I receive from those around me.
21. I communicate my thoughts and feelings with honesty and compassion.
22. I attract loving and supportive family relationships.
23. I deserve healthy boundaries in all my relationships.
24. I forgive myself and others, releasing any past hurts.
25. I am open to new connections and meaningful experiences.
26. I choose relationships that encourage personal growth and authenticity.
27. I value and nurture the relationships that bring me joy.
28. I attract people who uplift and inspire me to be my best self.
29. I am a loving and supportive partner for those I care about.

RELATIONSHIPS AND CONNECTION

30. I radiate love and kindness, creating a positive ripple effect in my relationships.
31. I let go of the need for external validation and find fulfillment in myself.
32. I attract friends who celebrate my uniqueness and support my dreams.
33. I deserve love and respect for all my relationships.
34. I cultivate deep and meaningful connections with others.
35. I embrace empathy and understanding in my interactions.
36. I communicate my desires and needs in a loving and assertive manner.
37. I attract romantic partners who bring out the best in me.
38. I create healthy and balanced dynamics in my relationships.
39. I attract people who appreciate and value me for who I am.
40. I am worthy of love and connection.
41. I release the need for perfection and embrace authentic connections.
42. I attract positive and uplifting friendships into my life.
43. I am open to giving and receiving support from my loved ones.
44. I choose relationships that inspire growth and happiness.
45. I attract relationships that are based on mutual trust and respect.
46. I deserve love and affection in my relationships.
47. I embrace the beauty of vulnerability and authentic connection.
48. I communicate my love and appreciation to those I care about.
49. I attract loving and nurturing partnerships in all areas of

my life.
50. I am surrounded by people who believe in me and my dreams.
51. I attract healthy and loving relationships effortlessly.
52. I choose partners who appreciate and celebrate my individuality.
53. I embrace healthy conflict resolution and effective communication.
54. I am open to receiving love and support from my loved ones.
55. I attract relationships that bring joy, growth, and fulfillment.
56. I deserve love and happiness in my romantic relationships.
57. I create space for deep and meaningful connections to thrive.
58. I choose relationships that align with my values and aspirations.
59. I attract friends who uplift and inspire me to be the best version of myself.
60. I radiate love and compassion, attracting positive connections into my life.
61. I deserve to love and nurture friendships.
62. I release fear and trust in the power of love to transform my relationships.
63. I communicate my needs and desires with confidence and clarity.
64. I attract partners who appreciate and cherish my unique qualities.
65. I am surrounded by loving and supportive family members.
66. I let go of toxic relationships and make room for healthy

connections.
67. I cultivate compassion and understanding in all my relationships.
68. I attract friendships that bring laughter, joy, and fulfillment.
69. I am open to experiencing deep emotional intimacy in my relationships.
70. I deserve love and acceptance, just as I am.
71. I choose relationships that encourage personal growth and self-expression.
72. I attract partners who celebrate and support my goals and dreams.
73. I communicate my boundaries and expectations with love and respect.
74. I am surrounded by people who uplift and inspire me.
75. I attract friendships that nourish and empower me.
76. I release the need for external validation and love myself unconditionally.
77. I am open to receiving and giving love freely.
78. I attract healthy and balanced relationships into my life.
79. I deserve love and affection in my relationships.
80. I choose partners who appreciate and honor my emotional needs.
81. I am worthy of experiencing deep and meaningful connections.
82. I attract friends who accept and appreciate me for who I am.
83. I communicate my feelings and desires with authenticity and courage.
84. I create space for open and honest communication in my relationships.

85. I am surrounded by loving and supportive individuals.
86. I attract partnerships that bring joy, growth, and fulfillment.
87. I embrace vulnerability as a strength in my relationships.
88. I deserve love and happiness in all my connections.
89. I attract friendships that inspire and uplift me.
90. I radiate love and positivity, attracting harmonious relationships.
91. I release the need for comparison and embrace the beauty of my unique journey.
92. I attract partners who value and respect my independence.
93. I communicate my love and appreciation to those who are dear to me.
94. I am open to giving and receiving love with an open heart.
95. I attract friendships that support and encourage my personal growth.
96. I choose relationships that bring out the best in me.
97. I deserve love and affection in my romantic partnerships.
98. I create a safe and loving environment for deep connection and intimacy.
99. I attract people who appreciate and celebrate my true essence.
100. I am worthy of experiencing love, joy, and fulfillment in my relationships.

7

Career and Professional Growth

Enter the powerful world of "Career and Professional Growth," where you'll discover your full potential, redefine success on your own terms, and embrace new prospects for growth and satisfaction. These affirmations will motivate you to follow your job goals with confidence, overcome challenges, and build a successful professional life that is connected to your passions and beliefs.

1. I can achieve great success in my career.
2. I embrace challenges as opportunities for growth and learning.
3. I have valuable skills and talents to offer in my profession.
4. I deserve recognition and advancement in my career.
5. I trust in my ability to handle any professional situation with grace and confidence.
6. I attract fulfilling and rewarding work opportunities.
7. I am focused and determined to achieve my career goals.
8. I am open to new possibilities and embrace change in my

professional life.
9. I create a positive and supportive work environment for myself and others.
10. I am a valuable asset to any team or organization.
11. I am constantly learning and developing in my professional journey.
12. I have the power to create a career path that aligns with my passions and values.
13. I trust my instincts and make decisions that lead to success.
14. I am confident in promoting my accomplishments and sharing my expertise.
15. I embrace networking as a way to expand my professional connections and opportunities.
16. I can overcome any obstacles that come my way.
17. I am worthy of receiving promotions, raises, and opportunities for growth.
18. I radiate professionalism and earn the respect of my colleagues and superiors.
19. I balance my work and personal lives, prioritizing self-care and well-being.
20. I am a leader, inspiring and empowering others with my actions and words.
21. I am resilient and bounce back from setbacks stronger than ever.
22. I attract mentors and role models who support my professional development.
23. I am confident in expressing my ideas and contributing to my unique perspective.
24. I embrace continuous learning and seek out new knowledge and skills.
25. I create a harmonious work-life balance that nourishes my

overall well-being.
26. I trust in my ability to make wise and strategic career choices.
27. I deserve recognition and rewards for my hard work and dedication.
28. I am grateful for the opportunities that come my way and make the most of them.
29. I approach challenges with creativity and resourcefulness, finding innovative solutions.
30. I am a trailblazer, breaking barriers and paving the way for others.
31. I am open to collaboration and value the contributions of others.
32. I embrace leadership opportunities and inspire those around me.
33. I am confident in presenting my ideas and asserting myself in professional settings.
34. I attract mentors and supporters who guide and advocate for my success.
35. I am committed to personal and professional growth, continuously improving myself.
36. I create a positive and supportive work environment where everyone can thrive.
37. I am worthy of financial abundance and prosperity in my career.
38. I am adaptable and embrace change as an opportunity for growth.
39. I trust my intuition to make career decisions that align with my values and purpose.
40. I am a role model, inspiring others with my achievements and work ethic.

41. I deserve opportunities for advancement and professional recognition.
42. I am skilled and competent in my field, earning the respect of others.
43. I attract fulfilling and purpose-driven work that brings me joy.
44. I am confident in my ability to handle any professional challenge that comes my way.
45. I am a lifelong learner, continuously expanding my knowledge and expertise.
46. I am focused and productive, making significant progress toward my career goals.
47. I celebrate my achievements and milestones along my career journey.
48. I radiate positivity and enthusiasm, creating a positive work environment.
49. I am deserving of work-life balance, nurturing both my personal and professional lives.
50. I am grateful for the opportunities that allow me to make a meaningful impact.
51. I am resilient and persevere through obstacles, emerging stronger and wiser.
52. I attract mentors and supporters who believe in my potential and offer guidance.
53. I am confident in promoting my unique skills and contributions in my field.
54. I am open to new possibilities and embrace growth opportunities in my career.
55. I trust myself to make wise decisions for my professional path.
56. I am respected and valued for my expertise and contribu-

tions.
57. I attract empowering and fulfilling work experiences.
58. I am a catalyst for positive change and progress in my industry.
59. I can balance multiple responsibilities and excel in each.
60. I am a visionary, seeing opportunities where others see challenges.
61. I deserve financial abundance and prosperity in my career.
62. I radiate confidence and charisma, leaving a lasting impression on others.
63. I embrace feedback as an opportunity for growth and improvement.
64. I am a problem-solver, finding creative solutions to complex challenges.
65. I attract opportunities that align with my passions and values.
66. I am an influential leader, inspiring and motivating others to reach their full potential.
67. I deserve respect and recognition for my contributions.
68. I am dedicated to continuous professional development and self-improvement.
69. I trust in my ability to navigate career transitions and embrace new beginnings.
70. I am an advocate for myself and others, promoting fairness and equality in the workplace.
71. I deserve promotions and advancements that reflect my skills and accomplishments.
72. I can achieve a fulfilling and successful career on my own terms.
73. I attract mentors and allies who support my professional growth and success.

74. I embrace challenges as opportunities to showcase my abilities and strengths.
75. I am confident in negotiating for what I deserve in my career.
76. I am a lifelong learner committed to staying ahead in my industry.
77. I attract meaningful and fulfilling collaborations and partnerships.
78. I deserve work that aligns with my purpose and passions.
79. I can achieve healthy work-life integration.
80. I am a catalyst for positive change in my organization and industry.
81. I am resourceful and find innovative solutions to obstacles.
82. I deserve a fulfilling and satisfying career journey.
83. I trust my intuition to guide me toward the right career opportunities.
84. I am a leader, empowering others to reach their full potential.
85. I attract mentors who provide guidance and support for my professional growth.
86. I am confident in my ability to navigate and adapt to changing career landscapes.
87. I deserve recognition for my unique contributions and talents.
88. I am focused and driven, taking deliberate steps toward my career goals.
89. I am grateful for the lessons and growth opportunities that come with my career.
90. I am a role model, inspiring others to pursue their passions and dreams.
91. I deserve work that brings me fulfillment and satisfaction.

92. I can overcome imposter syndrome and embrace my worthiness.
93. I attract opportunities that allow me to make a positive impact on others.
94. I am a lifelong learner, dedicated to acquiring new skills and knowledge.
95. I radiate confidence and professionalism in all my career endeavors.
96. I deserve success and achievements in my chosen career path.
97. I embrace challenges as opportunities for growth and self-discovery.
98. I can balance my professional aspirations with my personal life.
99. I am resilient and persevere through setbacks, emerging stronger and more determined.
100. I am the author of my career journey, and I choose to create a path filled with purpose, passion, and success.

8

Mindfulness and Emotional Well-being

Welcome to the chapter where you'll begin on a journey of self-discovery, inner peace, and emotional resilience. You will cultivate mindfulness, nurture your mental and emotional health, and discover harmony despite life's hardships by repeating these affirmations, generating a profound sense of well-being and peace.

1. I am present at this moment, embracing the beauty of now.
2. I release all worries and anxieties, allowing peace to flow through me.
3. I deserve love, compassion, and understanding.
4. I honor and nurture my emotional well-being every day.
5. I choose to let go of what no longer serves me, making space for positivity.
6. I am in control of my emotions, and I choose to respond with grace and kindness.
7. I trust the wisdom of my intuition to guide me in making

the right decisions.

8. I am grateful for the lessons that challenges bring as they help me grow.
9. I release all judgment towards myself and others, embracing acceptance.
10. I am worthy of self-care and prioritize my well-being in all aspects of my life.
11. I embrace the power of self-reflection and use it to cultivate personal growth.
12. I am gentle with myself during times of difficulty, knowing that I am doing my best.
13. I choose thoughts that empower and uplift me, replacing negativity with positivity.
14. I am resilient and have the strength to overcome any obstacle.
15. I let go of the past and live fully in the present moment.
16. I honor my emotions and allow myself to feel without judgment.
17. I deserve self-compassion and practice it daily.
18. I radiate love and positivity, attracting positive experiences and relationships.
19. I am in tune with my inner needs and give myself the care I deserve.
20. I am centered and grounded, finding peace within myself.
21. I release attachments to outcomes, trusting in the journey of life.
22. I embrace the beauty of imperfection and celebrate my unique self.
23. I forgive myself for past mistakes and embrace my journey of growth.
24. I surround myself with positive and uplifting energy.

25. I choose to see challenges as opportunities for learning and personal development.
26. I am grateful for the abundance of love and joy in my life.
27. I am connected to the present moment through my breath.
28. I release self-doubt and embrace my inner strength and confidence.
29. I trust in the process of life, knowing that everything unfolds in perfect timing.
30. I am open to receiving support and guidance from others when needed.
31. I release the need for validation from others and find validation within myself.
32. I am worthy of happiness, and I choose to create a life that brings me joy.
33. I let go of expectations and embrace the beauty of life's surprises.
34. I am in control of my thoughts, and I choose to focus on the positive.
35. I am resilient and bounce back from adversity with grace and strength.
36. I accept myself fully, including my flaws and imperfections.
37. I deserve rest and relaxation, and I prioritize self-care in my routine.
38. I let go of comparison and embrace my own unique journey.
39. I am at peace with my past, present, and future.
40. I am grateful for the lessons and growth that come from my experiences.
41. I release the need for perfection and allow myself to be human.
42. I trust in my ability to handle any challenge that comes my

way.
43. I attract positive and uplifting relationships into my life.
44. I deserve love, respect, and kindness from myself and others.
45. I let go of regret and embrace the power of forgiveness.
46. I am connected to my inner wisdom and trust in its guidance.
47. I am open to receiving and giving love freely.
48. I release the need for control and surrender to the flow of life.
49. I am worthy of success, and I have the skills and abilities to achieve my goals.
50. I am grateful for the simple joys and blessings in my life.
51. I let go of worry and trust in the universe's plan for me.
52. I am patient with myself and allow myself the time I need to heal and grow.
53. I radiate confidence and attract opportunities for growth and success.
54. I am a magnet for positive experiences and abundance.
55. I release any limiting beliefs that hold me back from reaching my full potential.
56. I deserve happiness and fulfillment in all areas of my life.
57. I choose to focus on the present moment, finding joy in the little things.
58. I am resilient and bounce back from setbacks with determination.
59. I am open to new possibilities and embrace change with grace.
60. I am at peace with myself and my journey, trusting in the process.
61. I deserve self-love and should treat myself with kindness

and compassion.
62. I release the need for approval from others and embrace my authentic self.
63. I am surrounded by love, support, and positive energy.
64. I let go of self-criticism and embrace self-acceptance.
65. I am grateful for my body and treat it with love and care.
66. I release stress and tension from my body and invite relaxation and calm.
67. I deserve happiness and fulfillment in my relationships.
68. I choose to let go of toxic relationships and surround myself with positive influences.
69. I am confident in expressing my needs and boundaries in relationships.
70. I deserve love and respect, and I attract healthy and fulfilling connections.
71. I trust my instincts and make decisions that align with my values and desires.
72. I am open to receiving and giving love and nurturing meaningful connections.
73. I let go of comparison and celebrate the uniqueness of my relationships.
74. I communicate openly and honestly in my relationships, fostering trust and understanding.
75. I deserve love and support, and I attract nurturing and supportive relationships.
76. I release the need for validation from others and find validation within myself.
77. I embrace vulnerability in my relationships, allowing for deeper connections.
78. I am a good listener and offer genuine support to those I care about.

79. I let go of past hurts and forgive myself and others in my relationships.
80. I am grateful for the love and connection I experience in my relationships.
81. I deserve success and fulfillment in my career.
82. I embrace my unique skills and talents, knowing they contribute value to my work.
83. I attract opportunities that align with my passions and goals.
84. I am confident in sharing my ideas and speaking up for myself in the workplace.
85. I embrace challenges as opportunities for growth and development in my career.
86. I deserve recognition and advancement in my professional life.
87. I cultivate a positive and supportive work environment for myself and others.
88. I am a valuable asset to my team and contribute to its success.
89. I let go of self-doubt and step into my power as a professional woman.
90. I am grateful for the opportunities and growth that my career brings.
91. I deserve balance and harmony between my work and personal life.
92. I am a competent professional, trusted in my field.
93. I attract mentors and colleagues who inspire and support my professional growth.
94. I am open to learning and expanding my skills in my career.
95. I embrace change and adaptability in my professional journey.

96. I deserve financial abundance and success in my career.
97. I set clear goals for myself and take consistent action to achieve them.
98. I am confident in my abilities to handle challenges and overcome obstacles in my career.
99. I create a meaningful impact through my work and contribute positively to society.
100. I am grateful for the opportunities and fulfillment that my career provides.

9

Personal Growth and Continuous Learning

Begin a new chapter of self-improvement and limitless potential with "Personal Growth and Continuous Learning." These affirmations will encourage you to accept progress, welcome change, and pursue lifelong learning, unlocking your full potential and opening doors to new possibilities and personal fulfillment.

1. I am committed to my personal growth and continuous learning journey.
2. I embrace challenges as opportunities for growth and self-improvement.
3. I am open to new experiences and stepping outside of my comfort zone.
4. I believe in my ability to learn and acquire new skills.
5. I am worthy of investing time and energy in my personal development.
6. I let go of self-limiting beliefs and embraced my full

potential.
7. I am constantly developing and becoming the best version of myself.
8. I am resilient and bounce back from setbacks with determination.
9. I seek knowledge and wisdom from a variety of sources.
10. I am committed to nurturing my mind, body, and soul for holistic growth.
11. I celebrate my progress and accomplishments, big and small.
12. I am open to feedback and use it as an opportunity for growth.
13. I create a supportive environment for my personal growth.
14. I set clear and achievable goals that align with my vision and values.
15. I believe in my ability to overcome challenges and achieve success.
16. I practice self-reflection and learn from my experiences.
17. I embrace change and adaptability as part of my personal growth journey.
18. I surround myself with positive and inspiring individuals who uplift me.
19. I deserve to invest in myself and my personal growth.
20. I am grateful for the lessons I have learned along my personal growth path.
21. I prioritize self-care and self-love as essential components of my personal growth.
22. I let go of perfectionism and embrace progress over perfection.
23. I trust my intuition to guide me on my personal growth journey.

PERSONAL GROWTH AND CONTINUOUS LEARNING

24. I am open-minded and willing to unlearn and relearn for personal growth.
25. I cultivate a growth mindset that allows me to learn from every situation.
26. I choose to see failures as opportunities for growth and learning.
27. I can break through self-imposed limitations.
28. I embrace self-discovery and uncovering my true passions and purpose.
29. I practice gratitude for the lessons and growth opportunities in my life.
30. I am dedicated to becoming the best version of myself every day.
31. I release the need for validation from others and trust my judgment.
32. I welcome challenges that push me outside of my comfort zone.
33. I am open to receiving guidance and mentorship on my personal growth journey.
34. I believe in my ability to overcome obstacles and achieve my goals.
35. I take responsibility for my own personal growth and development.
36. I am constantly learning and evolving, adapting to the ever-changing world.
37. I celebrate my uniqueness and embrace my individuality.
38. I am worthy of investing time and resources in my personal growth.
39. I am open to exploring new ideas and perspectives for personal growth.
40. I am grateful for the opportunities for personal growth

that come my way.
41. I choose to focus on solutions rather than dwelling on problems.
42. I am committed to developing healthy habits that support my personal growth.
43. I deserve love, compassion, and forgiveness on my personal growth journey.
44. I let go of comparison and embrace my path of personal growth.
45. I am dedicated to lifelong learning and improvement.
46. I embrace challenges as opportunities for self-discovery and personal growth.
47. I deserve to invest time and energy in my personal growth and well-being.
48. I release the fear of failure and embrace the lessons it brings.
49. I trust the process of my personal growth journey, knowing that it unfolds as it should.
50. I am grateful for the transformative power of personal growth in my life.
51. I choose to let go of the past and focus on the present moment for personal growth.
52. I am open to receiving support and guidance from others on my personal growth path.
53. I celebrate my progress and achievements, no matter how small.
54. I trust my inner wisdom to guide me on my personal growth journey.
55. I am dedicated to self-improvement and continuous learning.
56. I release the need for external validation and find valida-

tion from within.

57. I embrace challenges as opportunities for self-discovery and personal growth.
58. I am resilient and bounce back from setbacks with renewed strength.
59. I am committed to my personal growth, even when it feels uncomfortable.
60. I am grateful for the transformative power of personal growth in my life.
61. I let go of self-judgment and embrace self-acceptance on my personal growth journey.
62. I am open to new perspectives and ideas that contribute to my personal growth.
63. I trust that my personal growth journey is unfolding in perfect timing.
64. I am deserving of love, compassion, and self-care as I pursue personal growth.
65. I release the need for perfection and embrace the beauty of my imperfections.
66. I am dedicated to cultivating positive and empowering beliefs for personal growth.
67. I am open to learning from others and valuing their unique experiences.
68. I celebrate my progress and achievements, no matter how small they may seem.
69. I am committed to self-reflection as a tool for personal growth and self-awareness.
70. I am grateful for the lessons learned and growth experienced on my personal growth journey.
71. I embrace uncertainty as an opportunity for personal growth and transformation.

72. I trust my intuition to guide me on my personal growth journey.
73. I am open to expanding my comfort zone for personal growth and self-discovery.
74. I deserve to invest time, energy, and resources into my personal growth.
75. I release the need for external validation and seek validation from within.
76. I am resilient and bounce back from challenges with strength and determination.
77. I am committed to lifelong learning and self-improvement.
78. I celebrate my unique strengths and talents that contribute to my personal growth.
79. I am open to receiving feedback as a valuable tool for personal growth and improvement.
80. I am grateful for the opportunities for personal growth that come my way.
81. I let go of self-doubt and embrace self-belief in my personal growth journey.
82. I am open to exploring new interests and passions for personal growth and fulfillment.
83. I trust in my ability to handle any obstacles or challenges that arise on my personal growth journey.
84. I am committed to self-care and self-love as vital components of my personal growth.
85. I release the need for comparison and embrace my own unique path of personal growth.
86. I deserve to invest time and energy into my personal growth and well-being.
87. I celebrate the progress I have made and look forward to the growth that lies ahead.

PERSONAL GROWTH AND CONTINUOUS LEARNING

88. I trust in the process of personal growth, knowing that every step forward is valuable.
89. I am open to new opportunities and experiences that contribute to my personal growth.
90. I am grateful for the transformative power of personal growth in my life.
91. I choose to let go of fear and step into my personal growth with courage and confidence.
92. I am dedicated to developing empowering habits that support my personal growth.
93. I release the need for perfection and embrace the progress I make on my personal growth journey.
94. I am deserving of love, kindness, and self-compassion as I navigate my personal growth.
95. I embrace challenges as opportunities for self-discovery and personal growth.
96. I am open to receiving guidance and support from mentors and coaches on my personal growth journey.
97. I celebrate my unique journey and honor the growth I have achieved.
98. I trust in my own inner strength and resilience as I pursue personal growth.
99. I am committed to lifelong learning and expanding my knowledge for personal growth.
100. I am grateful for the continuous opportunities for personal growth and self-improvement in my life.

10

Balance and Well-being

Discover harmony and inner calm as you explore the revolutionary chapter "Balance and Well-being." These affirmations will lead you on a self-care journey, assisting you in prioritizing your physical, mental, and emotional well-being and encouraging you to live a balanced and fulfilled life.

1. I prioritize self-care and make time for my well-being.
2. I deserve balance and harmony in my life.
3. I listen to my body's needs and honor them with compassion.
4. I create a peaceful and nurturing environment for myself.
5. I find joy and fulfillment in simple moments of relaxation.
6. I release the need to control everything and trust in the flow of life.
7. I embrace a balanced approach to work, rest, and play.
8. I am open to receiving support and help when I need it.
9. I honor my boundaries and say no to what doesn't serve my well-being.

10. I am grateful for the abundance of love and positivity in my life.
11. I prioritize my mental and emotional health with kindness and care.
12. I nourish my body with wholesome foods and hydration.
13. I engage in activities that bring me joy and inspire my soul.
14. I find a balance between giving and receiving in all areas of my life.
15. I am in tune with my inner wisdom and trust my intuition.
16. I release stress and tension, allowing myself to relax and unwind.
17. I make self-care a non-negotiable part of my daily routine.
18. I surround myself with positive and uplifting energies.
19. I cultivate healthy and supportive relationships in my life.
20. I am grateful for the beauty and abundance of nature that nourishes my soul.
21. I prioritize quality sleep and create a restful environment for myself.
22. I engage in activities that bring me a sense of peace and calm.
23. I let go of perfectionism and embrace my authentic self.
24. I make time for activities that nurture my creative expression.
25. I release any guilt or self-judgment and embrace self-compassion.
26. I find a balance between work, family, and personal life.
27. I listen to my body's signals and give myself the care I need.
28. I create a healthy work-life balance that supports my well-being.
29. I practice mindfulness and live in the present moment.
30. I am grateful for the gift of life and cherish each day with

gratitude.
31. I cultivate a positive mindset and focus on uplifting thoughts.
32. I engage in regular exercise and movement that nourish my body.
33. I let go of comparison and embrace my unique journey.
34. I prioritize time for hobbies and activities that bring me joy.
35. I release the need for external validation and find validation within myself.
36. I create space for solitude and reflection to recharge my energy.
37. I make choices that align with my values and bring me peace.
38. I release negativity and choose to see the good in every situation.
39. I practice self-compassion and forgive myself for any perceived shortcomings.
40. I am grateful for my body's strength, resilience, and capacity for healing.
41. I find balance in giving and receiving love in my relationships.
42. I prioritize my own well-being without guilt or hesitation.
43. I trust in my ability to navigate challenges and find solutions.
44. I let go of stress and embrace a state of calm and serenity.
45. I create a balance between productivity and leisure in my life.
46. I honor my emotions and allow myself to feel and process them.
47. I surround myself with positive influences that uplift and

inspire me.
48. I practice gratitude for the blessings and abundance in my life.
49. I engage in practices that promote mental and emotional well-being.
50. I am grateful for the gift of life and embrace each moment with joy.
51. I cultivate healthy boundaries that protect my well-being.
52. I prioritize time for self-reflection and personal growth.
53. I am in tune with my body's needs and respond with love and care.
54. I release the need to please others and prioritize my own needs.
55. I nourish my mind, body, and soul with loving intentions.
56. I embrace change and see it as an opportunity for growth.
57. I choose thoughts and beliefs that support my well-being and happiness.
58. I am resilient and capable of overcoming any obstacles that come my way.
59. I deserve love, happiness, and abundance in all areas of my life.
60. I am grateful for the balance and harmony that exists within me and around me.
61. I trust in the process of life and surrender to its wisdom.
62. I embrace the power of positive affirmations to transform my life.
63. I create space for relaxation and rejuvenation in my daily routine.
64. I let go of self-doubt and step into my power and confidence.
65. I attract positive and fulfilling experiences into my life.

66. I am present in each moment, fully engaged and aware.
67. I make choices that align with my values and support my well-being.
68. I release the need for external validation and find validation within.
69. I deserve love, respect, and kindness in all my relationships.
70. I am grateful for the abundance of love and support in my life.
71. I release negative self-talk and replace it with self-affirming thoughts.
72. I prioritize activities that bring me joy, peace, and fulfillment.
73. I trust in my ability to handle whatever comes my way.
74. I nurture my body, mind, and soul with love and compassion.
75. I am in control of my happiness and create a life I love.
76. I choose to see challenges as opportunities for growth and transformation.
77. I surround myself with positive and supportive people.
78. I celebrate my achievements and acknowledge my progress.
79. I honor my emotions and express them in healthy and constructive ways.
80. I am grateful for the balance and harmony that exists in my life.
81. I embrace a holistic approach to well-being, nurturing all aspects of myself.
82. I trust my intuition to guide me in making empowered decisions.
83. I am resilient and capable of bouncing back from any

setbacks.
84. I create a sanctuary within myself where I can find peace and solace.
85. I practice self-care rituals that replenish my energy and uplift my spirit.
86. I release the need for comparison and focus on my own unique path.
87. I deserve success, abundance, and happiness in all areas of my life.
88. I attract positive opportunities and experiences into my life.
89. I am open to receiving love, support, and abundance from the universe.
90. I am grateful for the balance and well-being that flows through me.
91. I honor my need for rest and relaxation, allowing myself to recharge.
92. I trust that everything is unfolding for my highest good.
93. I cultivate a positive mindset and choose to empower thoughts.
94. I embrace the beauty of imperfection and embrace my authentic self.
95. I make choices that align with my values and bring me peace and fulfillment.
96. I create a harmonious work-life balance that supports my well-being.
97. I am grateful for the lessons and growth that come from challenging experiences.
98. I embrace self-reflection as a means of personal growth and self-discovery.
99. I am a beacon of light, radiating love, positivity, and well-

being.
100. I am the architect of my life, creating a beautiful balance of well-being and joy.

11

Gratitude and Abundance

This chapter may open your heart to the riches that surround you and build an attitude of thankfulness. You will learn to appreciate the benefits in your life, attract positivity, and adopt an abundant attitude that leads to more fulfillment and joy by using these affirmations.

1. I am grateful for the abundance that flows into my life.
2. I attract positive opportunities and experiences effortlessly.
3. I am open to receiving all the blessings the universe has in store for me.
4. I am worthy of love, joy, and abundance in all areas of my life.
5. I appreciate the beauty and miracles that surround me every day.
6. I am grateful for my body and all that it allows me to experience.
7. I am thankful for the relationships that bring love and

support into my life.
8. I am blessed with talents and skills that contribute to my success.
9. I am grateful for the lessons and growth that come from challenges.
10. I attract financial abundance and prosperity into my life.
11. I am thankful for the abundance of love and kindness in my life.
12. I am grateful for the opportunities that allow me to express my creativity.
13. I am surrounded by a loving and supportive community.
14. I appreciate the little things that bring me joy and happiness.
15. I am grateful for the abundance of opportunities for personal growth.
16. I attract positive and fulfilling relationships into my life.
17. I am thankful for the abundance of natural beauty in the world.
18. I am grateful for the abundance of health and well-being in my life.
19. I am blessed with a prosperous and fulfilling career.
20. I appreciate the abundance of time and resources available to me.
21. I am grateful for the abundance of knowledge and wisdom in the world.
22. I attract abundance and prosperity in alignment with my values.
23. I am thankful for the support and encouragement I receive from others.
24. I appreciate the abundance of joy and laughter in my life.
25. I am grateful for the opportunities to make a positive

impact in the world.
26. I am blessed with a loving and harmonious home.
27. I attract abundance and success in all my endeavors.
28. I am grateful for the abundance of peace and serenity in my life.
29. I am thankful for the abundance of opportunities for personal development.
30. I appreciate the abundance of natural resources that sustain me.
31. I am grateful for the abundance of opportunities to learn and grow.
32. I attract financial abundance and prosperity with ease and grace.
33. I am blessed with abundant energy and vitality.
34. I am grateful for the abundance of love and support from my family.
35. I am thankful for the abundance of beauty and inspiration in the world.
36. I appreciate the abundance of opportunities to contribute and make a difference.
37. I attract abundance and success in all areas of my life.
38. I am grateful for the abundance of creativity and inspiration within me.
39. I am blessed with abundant opportunities to travel and explore.
40. I appreciate the abundance of peace and tranquility in my life.
41. I am grateful for the abundance of joy and happiness that fills my days.
42. I attract abundance and prosperity by aligning with my purpose.

43. I am thankful for the abundance of supportive and uplifting friendships.
44. I appreciate the abundance of love and kindness I receive from others.
45. I am grateful for the abundance of opportunities for personal fulfillment.
46. I am blessed with an abundant and loving heart.
47. I attract abundance and success effortlessly and naturally.
48. I am grateful for the abundance of opportunities to connect with nature.
49. I am thankful for the abundance of positive and empowering thoughts.
50. I appreciate the abundance of time to pursue my passions and dreams.
51. I am grateful for the abundance of gratitude that fills my heart.
52. I attract financial abundance and wealth into my life.
53. I am blessed with an abundance of creativity and imagination.
54. I am grateful for the abundance of love and appreciation in my life.
55. I am thankful for the abundance of opportunities to learn and grow.
56. I appreciate the abundance of support and guidance available to me.
57. I attract abundance and success by embracing my true worth.
58. I am grateful for the abundance of peace and harmony in my relationships.
59. I am blessed with an abundance of inner strength and resilience.

60. I appreciate the abundance of opportunities to make a positive impact.
61. I am grateful for the abundance of wisdom and intuition within me.
62. I attract financial abundance and prosperity through my talents.
63. I am thankful for the abundance of joy and laughter shared with loved ones.
64. I appreciate the abundance of positive affirmations that uplift my spirit.
65. I am grateful for the abundance of opportunities to connect with others.
66. I am blessed with an abundant and fulfilling career.
67. I attract abundance and success by aligning with my passions.
68. I am grateful for the abundance of opportunities to practice self-care.
69. I am thankful for the abundance of love and support from the universe.
70. I appreciate the abundance of miracles and synchronicities in my life.
71. I am grateful for the abundance of compassion and empathy within me.
72. I attract financial abundance and prosperity by embracing abundance mindset.
73. I am blessed with an abundance of health and vitality.
74. I am grateful for the abundance of inspiration and creativity in the world.
75. I am thankful for the abundance of opportunities to serve others.
76. I appreciate the abundance of peace and serenity in my

mind and heart.
77. I attract abundance and success by believing in my limitless potential.
78. I am grateful for the abundance of opportunities to practice self-love.
79. I am blessed with an abundance of supportive and nurturing relationships.
80. I appreciate the abundance of opportunities to express my authentic self.
81. I am grateful for the abundance of gratitude that radiates from my being.
82. I attract financial abundance and prosperity by aligning with my purpose.
83. I am thankful for the abundance of beauty and inspiration in the world.
84. I appreciate the abundance of opportunities to learn and grow each day.
85. I am grateful for the abundance of love and connection in my life.
86. I am blessed with an abundance of clarity and focus in my endeavors.
87. I attract abundance and success by embracing my unique gifts and talents.
88. I am grateful for the abundance of opportunities to contribute to others.
89. I am thankful for the abundance of support and encouragement in my journey.
90. I appreciate the abundance of joy and happiness that fills my days.
91. I am grateful for the abundance of love and kindness that surrounds me.

92. I attract financial abundance and wealth by aligning with abundance consciousness.
93. I am blessed with an abundance of energy and vitality to pursue my dreams.
94. I am grateful for the abundance of opportunities to learn and expand my knowledge.
95. I am thankful for the abundance of possibilities and potential in every moment.
96. I appreciate the abundance of peace and harmony that flows through my life.
97. I attract abundance and success by embracing a positive mindset.
98. I am grateful for the abundance of opportunities to practice self-compassion.
99. I am blessed with an abundance of love and support from the universe.
100. I appreciate the abundance of miracles and blessings that manifest in my life.

12

Conclusion

As we reach the end of this book, "1000 Positive Affirmations for Women," I hope you have a refreshed sense of empowerment and a strong connection to your inner strength. Throughout this book, we have explored the vast area of affirmations, covering all parts of your life and inviting you to embrace your full potential.

Remember, you have the power to change your life. By implementing these affirmations into your daily routine, you've taken an important step toward living a life full of love, confidence, and plenty. Allow these affirmations to serve as a beacon, a constant reminder of your greatness and the endless possibilities that await you.

Remember that self-compassion and patience are essential as you continue on your path of personal development. Allow yourself to change and embrace the process of self-discovery, understanding that each affirmation you repeat and embody shapes your reality. Trust your inner knowledge and intuition

CONCLUSION

to lead you down the road that is true to your real self.

Use these affirmations as effective tools to change your perspective and navigate through adversity when you confront challenges and barriers along the path. Allow them to block self-doubt and criticism, reminding you of your inner strength, resilience, and merit.

Remember that the process of personal development is ongoing. Revisit this book as you continue to develop and progress, garnering inspiration and wisdom whenever you need it. Allow these affirmations to weave their way into your being, changing your perception of yourself and the world around you.

May the affirmations in this book continue to lead you to a life of love, acceptance of yourself, and abundance. You are an extraordinary woman, and the world is eager to experience the magic you contain within.

www.ingramcontent.com/pod-product-compliance
Lightning Source LLC
Chambersburg PA
CBHW050446010526
44118CB00013B/1698